the 9-life habits of
Highly Effective Cats

Thorsons
An imprint of HarperCollins Publishers
77-85 Fulham Palace Road,
Hammersmith, London W6 8JB

The Thorsons website address is: www.thorsons.com

First published in Great Britain by Thorsons 2001

10 9 8 7 6 5 4 3 2 1

Text and Illustrations © Margaret Woodhouse 2001

Margaret Woodhouse asserts the moral right to be
identified as the author of this work

A catalogue record of this book is available from the British Library

ISBN 0-00-712 348 5

Printed in Hong Kong

the 9-life habits of
Highly
Effective
Cats

Margaret Woodhouse

Thorsons

For Jack

The 9-Life Frame of Mind

▲▲▲▲▲▲▲

Congratulations!

You are about to become a highly effective cat. You will already be aware of your 9-Life status. Every cat *knows* it has 9 lives. But you should neither abuse nor neglect these lives. They can be over in 9 shakes of a tail if you do.

The 9-Life Habits give you the tools to maintain your lives for as long as possible. Practised consistently, they will lead you to a happy, healthy, 18–year plus life, free from responsibility and care.

Start your journey to feline purrfection by looking in the mirror. Bewildered? You are indeed-in-need of a 9-Life make-over.

There are 9 hallmarks of a well-versed, highly effective cat. For the cat who has the 9-Life knowledge, these attributes come naturally. You will observe them on the following pages. Study them carefully.

1. Sharpened claws.

2. Keen hearing.

3. Flat-ear flexibility.

4. Full fat tails.

5. An ability to puff up in size.

6. Expressive body curves.

7. An ability to move quickly.

8. A knowledge of heights

9. And an in-built alarm system.

HABIT 1
The Power Catnap

▲▲▲▲▲▲▲

Now it's time to teach yourself the 9-Life Habits. The first is to know the correct way to sleep. Sleep is an essential part of being an effective cat.

Note the following sleep positions:

Position 1

This position is suitable for sound sleeping. At these times you need to use your whole brain. Whole brain sleep is a simple energy reviver.

Position 2

Results from sleeping in Position 2 will be similar to those in Position 1.

Position 3

A semi-brain sleep state is also possible and efficacious. This is known as catnapping.

Position 4

Of all the sleep poses, that shown in Position 4 is the most effective. Alert for possible food or danger, yet in repose for maximum energy replacement, this is known as the *Power Catnap*. This is the sleep of the truly effective cat.

Whichever sleep position you choose, be positive. Examples of
positive sleep language are:

"I choose this sofa for my afternoon kip."

"I prefer sun to shade."

"I will stay here for some time."

"This box looks to be the perfect shape for snoozing in."

Adopt this sleep maxim:

There can be no power without sleep.

Too often cats use sleep simply as a means to while away the daylight hours. This is hardly *highly* effective.

Your goal is to maximise your 9 lives. *Power catnap* and be ready for any occasion.

At the end of a sleep, practise the following exercises for inner wellbeing.

Step 1...

and 2

9-LIFE HABIT 1 TAUGHT YOU THAT SEMI-BRAIN SLEEP PROLONGS YOUR 9 LIVES AND MAKES YOU A HIGHLY SUCCESSFUL CAT.

HABIT 2
The Wash

▲▲▲▲▲▲▲

Getting clean is but a small part of the washing function. Washing produces extreme effectiveness. It lets you to turn embarrassment into victory. Examples of positive wash language are:

"I've been caught in the flower bed – I must wash."

"The bird flew off – I must wash."

"I missed the ledge – I must wash."

"Uh-oh, my tail is in the bowl – I must wash."

Adopt this wash maxim:

Physical flexibility is the route to psychological dexterity.

The following exercises help you develop the physical flexibility
you will need to wash. Once limber, an effective cat will have the
psychological advantage for every occasion.

Wash Exercise 1

Resting on back with forepaws in support, wash the back legs.

Wash Exercise 2

In 'cello' position and using right
forepaw for principal support,
wash tail.

Wash Exercise 3

Effect a scissors action with back
legs and wash from top of thigh
down to each pad.

You will note the fine-tuned balance of each exercise. Balance of this
kind is learnt only through persistent practice.

For maximum effectiveness it is important to avoid washing-on-the-edge. A loss of composure is *very definitely not* highly effective (*see below*).

Learn to wash for every eventuality and you will remain strong and composed.

And don't forget to conserve some of that 9-Life-giving energy. Wash with a friend.

9-LIFE HABIT 2 TAUGHT YOU THAT WASHING HELPS YOU TO BE MORE COMPOSED IN YOUR LIVES AND MAKES YOU A HIGHLY SUCCESSFUL CAT.

HABIT 3
Picky Eating
▲▲▲▲▲▲

The highly effective cat must appear ambivalent about food. Ambivalence means knowing that you may or may not choose to eat what is put in front of you.

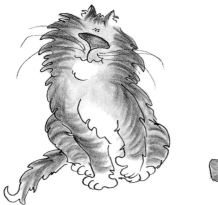

Your picky eating habits will help to intensify your resident human's anxiety, making them more controllable. You will find that being

ambivalent also delivers a greater culinary choice and increased overall dietary satisfaction.

The following are the classic features of a picky eater:

1. Full tummy.
2. Empty head.
3. A tail which says, "I won't say 'no', but don't be disappointed if I don't say 'yes'."

Cats who are picky eaters run rings round their resident humans. As you can see, they are highly effective cats.

Adopt these resident human-control techniques:

Technique 1

Eat two mouthfuls with gusto, then abandon the meal by appearing not to notice that anything was provided in the first place.

Technique 2

When presented with rotisserie chicken or similar delicacy devour your portion immediately then weave back for second and third helpings – even if your hunger is sated.

Technique 3

When the fridge door is opened, head towards it with an urgency then ignore the snack that is provided as a consequence.

Each one of these techniques adds uncertainty to your resident human's understanding of your eating habits.

Be warned, should you no longer be a picky eater you may never be able to dictate your diet again.

9-LIFE HABIT 3 TAUGHT YOU THAT BEING PICKY ABOUT FOOD PREVENTS WHISKER RASH IN YOUR LIVES AND MAKES YOU A HIGHLY SUCCESSFUL CAT.

You and Your Resident Human

▲▲▲▲▲▲▲▲

It is very important to bond with your resident human and enjoy this happiest of interfaces. Do not worry that you may compromise your aloofness. Resident humans are without sanity when it comes to their cats. This interdependent relationship can be a mutually satisfactory, highly effective one.

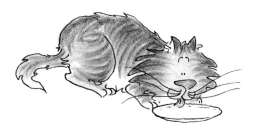

Resident humans are also an excellent source of food.

Adopt this sensible food maxim:
Clean kill is kinder to the resident human.

If you must take home your kill, it is highly effective behaviour to
ensure that it has been well sanitised first.

unsanitised kill

sanitised kill

Employ the following strategies to make the kill seem more sanitary.

1. Treat the kill as a gift. (Your resident human will consider this in mitigation.)
2. Limit the amount of kill you inflict on any one occasion.
3. Try not to include entrails.
4. Your resident human may be more tolerant of one kind of kill than another. Learn to tell which is which.
5. The placing of kill is of the utmost importance.
6. Try not to crunch your kill in resident human bedrooms in the middle of the night.

9-Life Habit 4 helps you to balance life with your resident human.

Too much *dependence* on your resident human makes you a pussy cat
    rather than a highly effective cat. This may give you a great sense
    of private victory but you will end up with fur balls.

Too much *independence* and you will find yourself working harder
    than any self-respecting feline needs to.

Aim instead for the well-balanced public victory that *interdependence*
    offers. You will satisfy your primordial needs, yet still enjoy a
    free lunch (*see graph opposite*).

INTERDEPENDENCE
"I'll bring home a bird so that she feeds me some canned food in the vain hope that I will not do it again."

She has guests
for dinner…

PUBLIC VICTORY

bring a dead bird into
the living room
(cleaned & gutted).

INDEPENDENCE
"I'll go out and kill my own food – and eat it."

You've had a
good night on the tiles…

PRIVATE VICTORY

leave a dead
bird in the bathroom
(entrails partially exposed).

DEPENDENCE
"Who needs to hunt when there's a can in the cupboard."

Your Mission is to live in harmony with your resident human. Each morning say the following to yourself:

"To fulfil this mission I will
        learn to weave,
        strike beguiling poses,
        purr on demand."

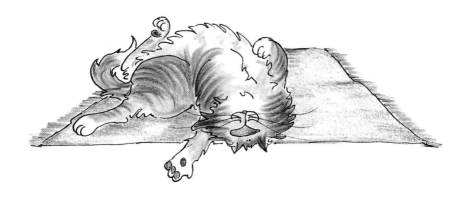

Adopt this human relationship maxim:
Refrain from disdain towards your resident human.

Your food source must never be treated with disdain. That should be
reserved for strangers and dangers. Instead, adopt these excellent
strategies for a premium resident human response.

1. To enter the house, present only part of your face at the window.

2. Do forward rolls with last minute retractions.

3. Place your head on cute angles.

4. Hurtle about in indiscriminate fashions.

5. And don't be afraid to reveal the softer side of your nature.

9-LIFE STRATEGY 6 TAUGHT YOU THAT NURTURING YOUR RESIDENT HUMAN PUTS BACK THE PURR IN YOUR LIVES AND MAKES YOU A HIGHLY SUCCESSFUL CAT.

HABIT 5
Creative Behaviour and Dogs
▲▲▲▲▲▲▲▲

There is but one highly effective way to deal with dogs – using coercion. Restraint and constraint are your allies, your tools.

Thus, when faced with a dog you must be both reactive and pro-active. Stay well in control while inflicting maximum damage on the dog's reputation.

Examples of reactive–pro-active language are:

Example 1.

Step A. "Here comes that cat-chasing dog."

Step B. "I will take an escape route my
resident human may notice."

Example 2.

Step A. "Here comes that cat-food eating
dog."

Step B. "I will use language my resident
human may notice."

Used correctly, your resident human will be invaluable in warding off dogs. The following postures will alert them to inappropriate dog behaviour.

Dog Defence Step 1

Withdraw chin deeply into chest while leaving forepaws in ready-to-spring position.

Dog Defence Step 2

Make your way immediately to prearranged assembly point. Do not
  run.

Dog Defence Step 3

Opening your mouth in a constrained,
  stifled position, emit a continuous I-
  have-a-live-rescuable-bird-in-my-
  mouth noise. This will bring your
  resident human running.

Adopt this dog maxim:

You make every difference by showing indifference.

It is most effective when exposed to a dog to treat it with an air of indifference.

An air of indifference looks like this.

By seeming indifferent, you will give the impression that you do not care whether the dog eats you or not – indicating that it takes more than a bark to twist your whisker. This will paralyse any self-respecting dog, making you a most effective dog-deflecting cat.

The following are the classic features of a dog-deflecting cat:

1. Never-you-care front paws.
2. On-the-ready back paws.
3. A tail which says, "The danger is present, but I'll keep up the flicks till the danger is past."

Cats who show that they are indifferent to dogs are displaying calm in the face of adversity. They are highly effective cats.

But do remember, there are advantages to be gained from recognising the odd-dog exception.

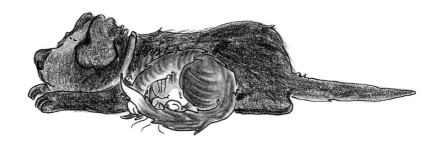

9-LIFE STRATEGY 5 TAUGHT YOU THAT BEING THE ONE IN CONTROL AROUND DOGS PRESERVES YOUR LIVES AND MAKES YOU A HIGHLY SUCCESSFUL CAT.

Disarm Unwanted Visitors
▲▲▲▲▲▲▲

The 6th habit is how to disarm unwanted visitors. When a stranger visits it is time to display disdain. Disdain is an essential part of being an effective cat.

The following expressions exude disdain from every paw:

Expression 1

This expression is suitable for first-time visitors. Keep an even distance between yourself and the visitor at all times.

Expression 2

This disdainful expression is
    particularly effective when
    greeting timid visitors.

The stylish method of puffing up your fur to its fullest while
    appearing aloof is known as *coat hauteur.*

Expression 3

Perhaps a little more basic,
    expression 3 will nonetheless
    get the message across with
    startling effect.

Adopt this unwanted visitor maxim:

The dagger is in the eyes.

If the unwanted visitor returns, it is time to perpetuate the *Narrow Eye Myth*. Humans believe cats are drawn to people who greet them with narrowed eyes. Thus, when the cat-hater narrows their eyes in distaste at a cat, the cat assumes friendship and will sit on their lap.

This is a myth. Any pussy cat can pick a cat-hater. But there is no better way to ensure the cat-hater departs permanently than by snuggling in and leaving fur *all over* their clothes.

Highly effective!

Try this excellent parting gesture, best delivered once you have got the unwanted visitor on the move.

9-LIFE HABIT 6 TAUGHT YOU THAT ESCHEWING VISITORS ENSURES BALANCE IN YOUR LIVES AND MAKES YOU A HIGHLY SUCCESSFUL CAT.

High Tails and Human Children
▲▲▲▲▲▲▲

We cannot emphasise enough the need to deflect attention away from yourself when a young human child is near. The following pictures may be distressing, but heed their warning.

Outcome to avoid 1

You are sitting obliging a child with your purring but you prove too cute. They decide to put you in the pram…

Outcome to avoid 2

You have simply made the mistake of taking a whole brain sleep instead of *power catnapping*. (Please don't forget! Power catnapping is the essential sleep position around children. It allows for a composed escape.)

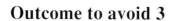

Outcome to avoid 3

You are walking through the house minding your own business but not sufficiently aware of the child coming up behind you…

Adopt this child maxim:

High tailing is the way to go.

The following postures prove highly effective in deflecting children.
Remember the golden rule; walk quickly, don't run.

Hiding from the human child can be highly effective. However, remember to include your extremities in the concealment.

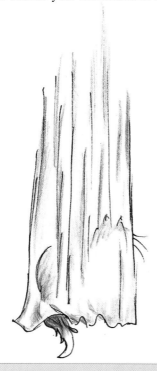

9-LIFE HABIT 7 TAUGHT YOU THAT AVOIDING HUMAN CHILDREN SAFEGUARDS YOUR LIVES AND MAKES YOU A HIGHLY SUCCESSFUL CAT.

In Purrsuit of the Inner Kitten

▲▲▲▲▲▲▲

9-Life Habit 4 taught you to nurture your resident human. Habit 8 teaches you to nurture yourself. Nurturing yourself is an essential part of being an effective cat.

Note the following nurturing purrsuits:

Purrsuit 1

This activity is ideal following a good feed. By electrifying your spirit you derive a double energy store, first from your food then from your frolic.

Purrsuit 2

The ultimate recreational pastime, this
    activity is ideal for the kitten learning
    effective habits early. Mature kittens will
    find this habit effective also.*

Purrsuit 3

Use either an appropriate toy or your human
    resident's hand and rotate your back legs
    rapidly. Desist if the toy or hand becomes
    shredded.

*For a more detailed disquisition on purring see *Know Your Cat's Purr Points*

Purrsuit 4

For this activity you need a friend. Entice them under a sheet of newspaper. Just as your vitality reaches its zenith, pounce. You will be thrilled at how far your effectiveness has taken you and your friends will find you full of *purrlure*.

On no account should your purrsuits allow you to lose composure. Do not forget the lessons learned from Habit 2, and be particularly cautious on wooden floors.

9-LIFE HABIT 8 TAUGHT YOU THAT PLAY ENERGISES YOUR LIVES AND MAKES YOU A HIGHLY SUCCESSFUL CAT.

HABIT 9
Sharpen Your Claw

▲▲▲▲▲▲▲

Habit 9 is the habit that makes all other habits possible. Without a
   sharp claw you cannot be sure you have the advantage. Having
   sharp claws is an essential part of being an effective cat.

The following honing skills will take your effectiveness to the 9th
   and ultimate level:

Honing skill 1

Arrive at window sill with
   your back legs still
   unsecured. Clamber up.

Honing skill 2

Lie on your back alongside the rear of sofa. Progress in an energetic backstroke from one end to the other.

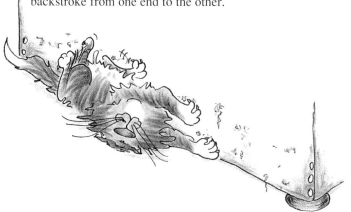

Honing skill 3

Place back legs in well supported position and casually rake the carpet. (Fine woven carpets provide the most effect.)

Adopt this sharp claw maxim:

It is better to be safe than sorry.

It is permissible and, of course, the epitome of effectiveness to use
your sharp claws in self-defence…

but draw the line at exercising Habit 9 too intensively in the presence of your resident human.

9-LIFE HABIT 9 TAUGHT YOU THAT IF ALL ELSE FAILS SHARP CLAWS WILL ALWAYS MAKE YOU A HIGHLY SUCCESSFUL CAT.